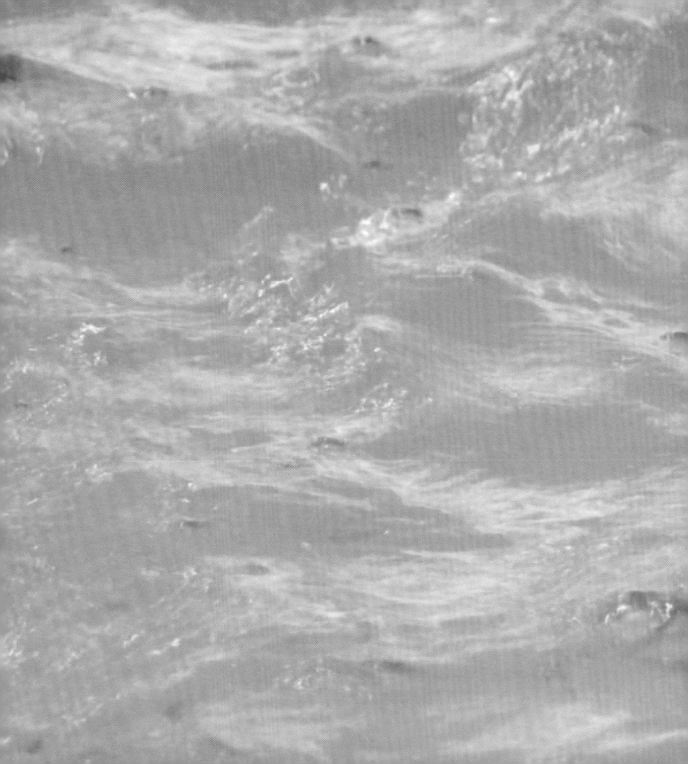

diving in

by rachel awes

all i did was listen also available by rachel awes
+ endorsed by SARK and kelly rae roberts.

diving in
isbn 978-1-4675-9830-9

2014 first edition

copyright © 2014 by rachel awes

all i did was listen
p.o. box 4422
saint paul, mn 55104
usa

www.rachelawes.com
rachelawes@gmail.com

printed in the united states of america by signature book printing.
www.sbpbooks.com

diving in

by rachel awes

this book is for the dolphins. for the whales + waves + sea. this book is for the water in the you + in the me. this book is for the movement of expanse + stretch + free.

diving in, rachel

"why are you standing way over there?", asked the water. "i am watching you", i replied. the water rose up + made sure i heard what she had to say next: "i am not separate from you. i am your life. you are made up of water. you are brimming with movement that terrifies you + material that electrifies you. now throw off your sandals + dive in. drench yourself in all your stories. meet yourself in the middle. come alive. swim, my dearest dear, swim".

+ so i do the only thing
  i can do, because i live
+ breathe in relationship.
          i respond...

one of my least favorite
field trips is the search
for a new swim suit.

i want one where the
colors + design bring
Out the brightest in me

+ i don't want what might put
my least flattering views on

LOUDSPEAKER. mostly, i want
a Kind Suit that suits me ✻

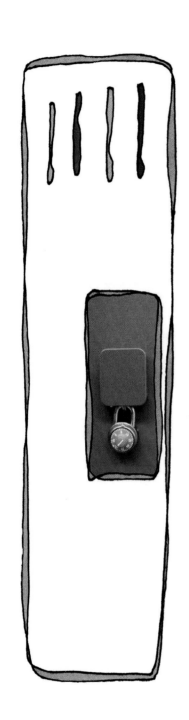

i am self-conscious
as i undress in the
locker room. bare
before others + they
before me, bareness
seems a requirement,
a prerequisite. a
way i must go
if i am to dive
into water + swim.*

i stand at the edge of
the pool. ready to dive
in. Knowing the water
will greet me with chill
+ shock + awakening.
Knowing i want in.

Knowing i want to
feel all of it ✿

i submerge into the water. i am a hippy submarine with flowers + rainbows + free to move forward.

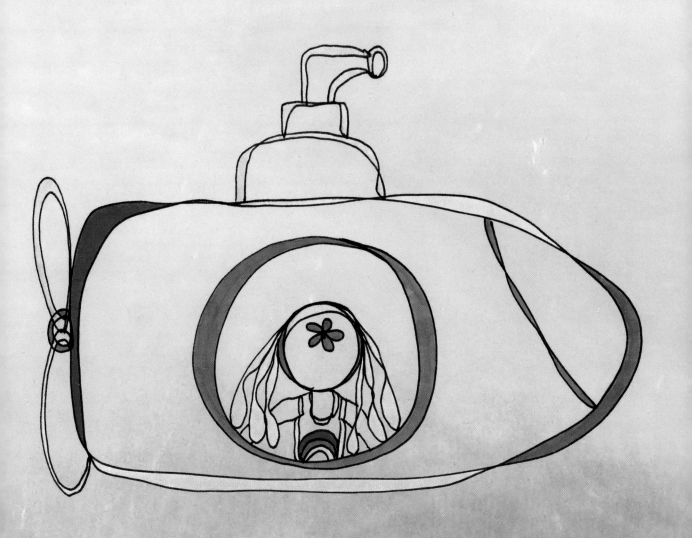

i watch the other swimmers
+ await instruction. . .
something always comes.
this time it is the butterfly.
someone is swimming it.
he doesn't know his secret
is out. winged ones are
just above the waters
surface

they are right next to me.
right next to us all ✼

i watch my hand glide
forward in the pool as i swim.

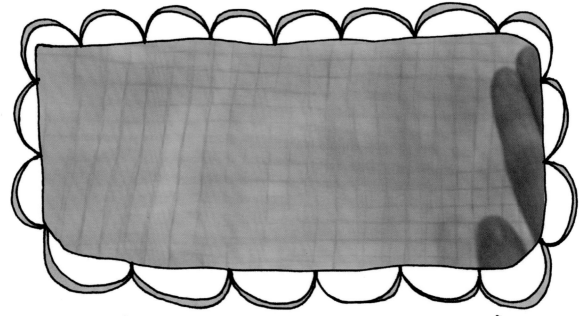

there isn't much else to see in
such a place. left hand, right.
over + over. a simple meditation.
moving through this world.
my life. me ✻

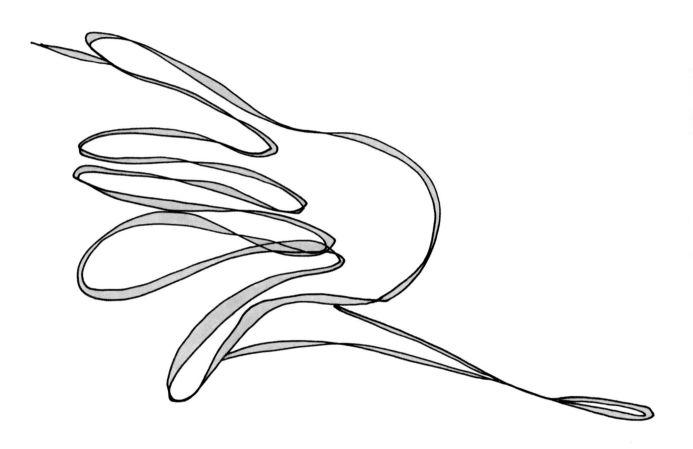

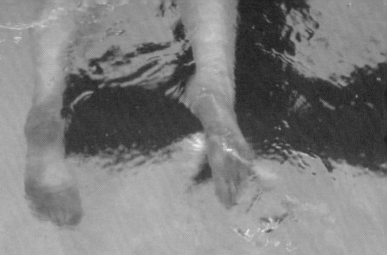

i watch the shallow water
turn into the deep end
+ i realize my task is
still the same. put
one arm in front of the next
+ keep kicking + breathing
+ moving forward ✲

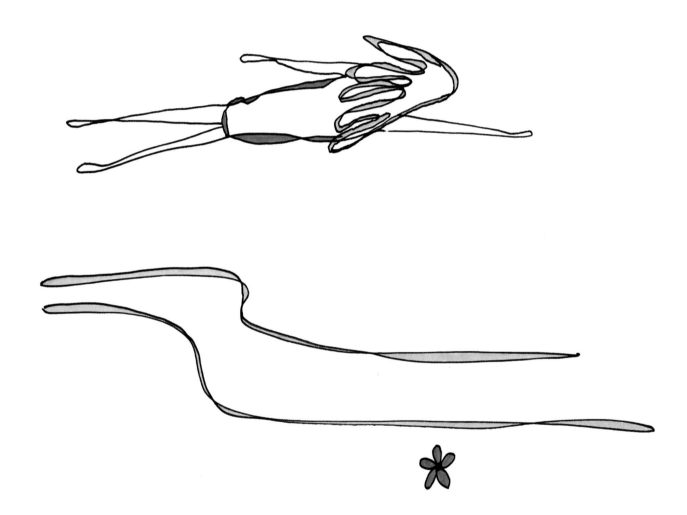

my mind thinks simple
thoughts in my opening
laps. Keeping count.
seeing square patterns
on the pool floor. more
inspired thoughts seem to
come toward the middle
+ the end. this encourages
me to not give up. to
keep kicking. loveliness
shows up when i do.
eventually ✳

✳   ✳

today i imagined a dolphin
swimming beside me. a
new friend. we didn't
need to say anything +
glanced at each other
often. maybe somewhere
in the deeps a dolphin
is imagining me too.
maybe more is possible
in this water than i
ever let myself see *

i told myself i was
moving toward
my dreams
as i
swam. closer +
closer with every
stroke. then i
realized it is never
about toward. it is
about in. . . . .

my dreams are in the whole pool

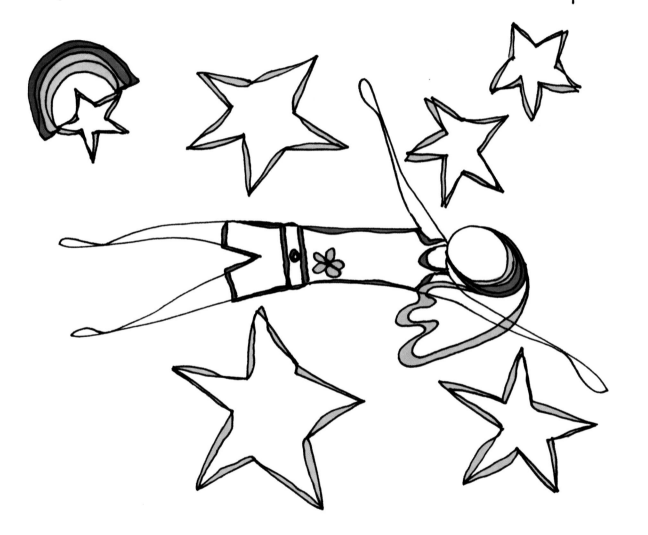

+ i am swimming in them *

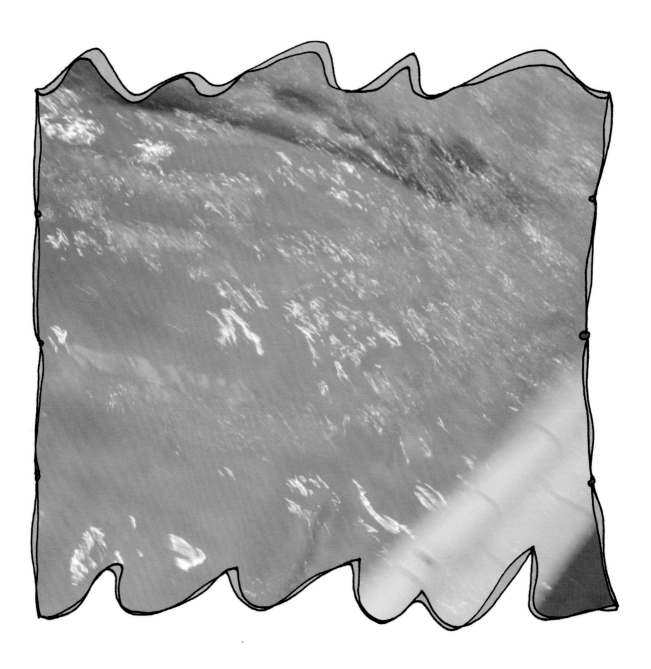

people swimming in other
lanes are creating waves

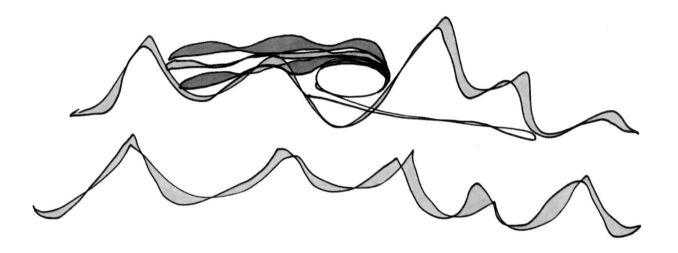

that are making the water
choppier + harder to move through❁

i had the whole pool to myself. the expanse was freeing + i believed i could stretch into all of it. then people started to get in + i could feel myself shrink back, until i remembered that whales don't concern themselves with these kinds of things. the water is always big enough for us, no matter what is going on inside it ✳

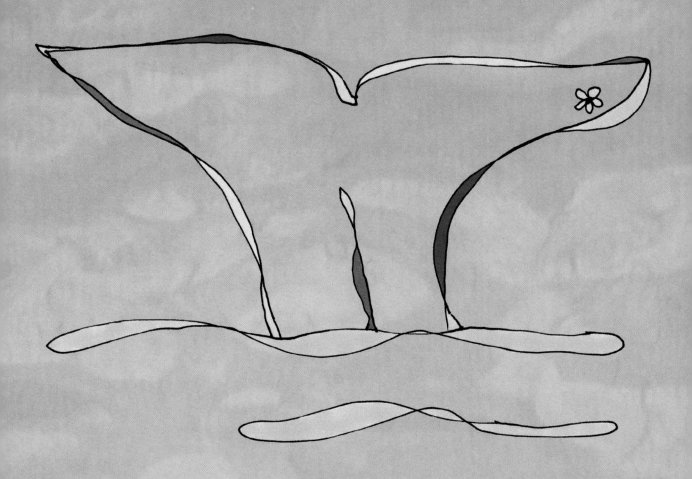

i stop at the end of some laps to take a breath. to huff + puff. to re-gain strength. for the next lap + the next. because i want to rise for all of it. because i can🌸

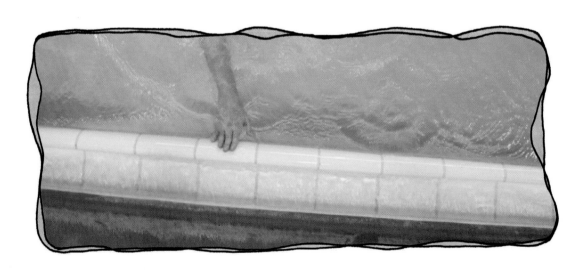

i like to clear my
goggles of all water
+ fog so i can see
all the way to
the bottom ✳

i held my breath + my face
turned into the water + i
saw someone swimming in
the way under. his body
was moving like a wave.
a wave in the water beneath
the water. in the almost unseen.

so beautiful in the deeps.
of course this is how it
really is ✤

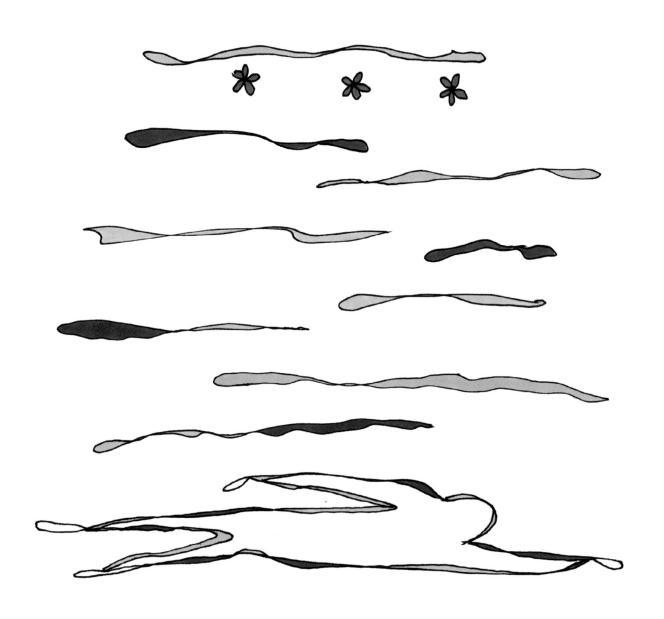

today's swim was all about thank yous. at the turn of each lap it was thank you to beaches of agates, deer, bunnies, solitude, poetry books... i could have swam this way for a long, long time. maybe this is what gratitude does. it keeps us going ✿

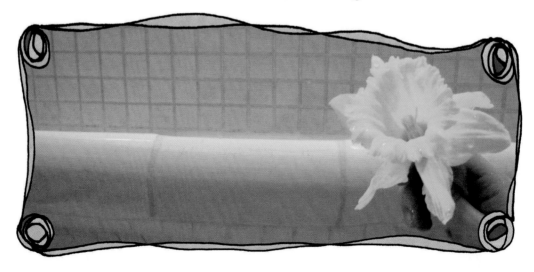

stretching my arms further.
feeling the pull in my
middle. allowing growing
pains to be here. reaching
into their farthest reaches,
but not so far that there's
pain. far enough to feel
what there is to feel +
be what there is to be. ✽

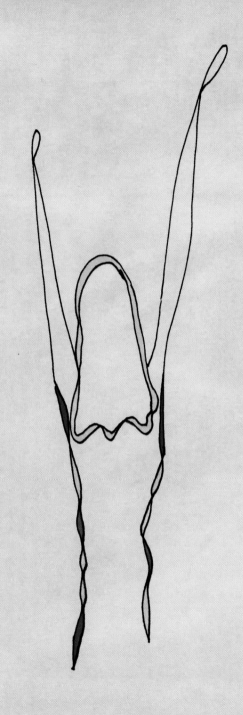

the colors i fill in at the edge of my body. around my hair. throughout the water. they are real, you know. my beauty is really real *

46

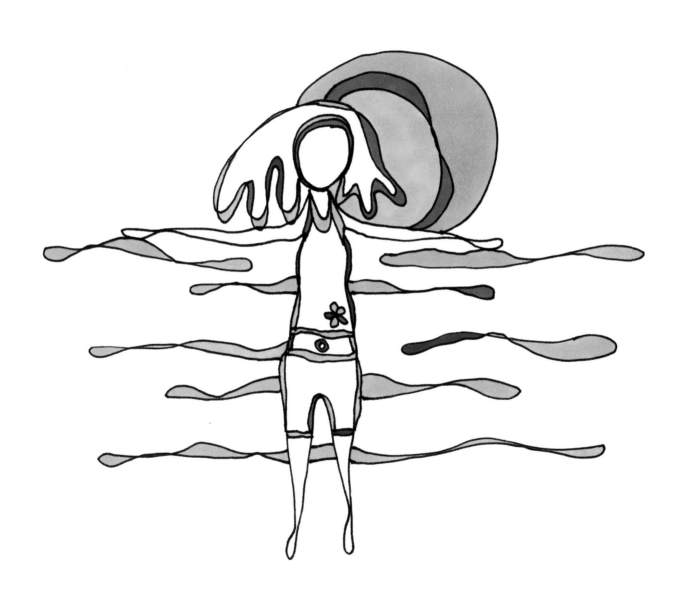

i have always swam with only turning my face to the right side to breathe + today, i began something new. i turned to the right + left to breathe. it was uncomfortable to change. fear spoke + said this could take me under. . . . .

of course this is how it's
always done.

some part of me needs
to die a little in order
to live a little more. ✽

i relaxed my head
more deeply into
the water as i swam.
i want to remember
to rest not only when
i stop but also as i
go *

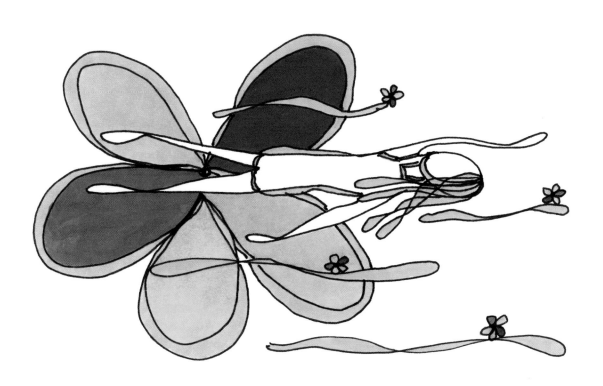

into my suit + water +
swimming. again + again.
into + into. i don't want
to stop. i don't want
to give up on me ✿

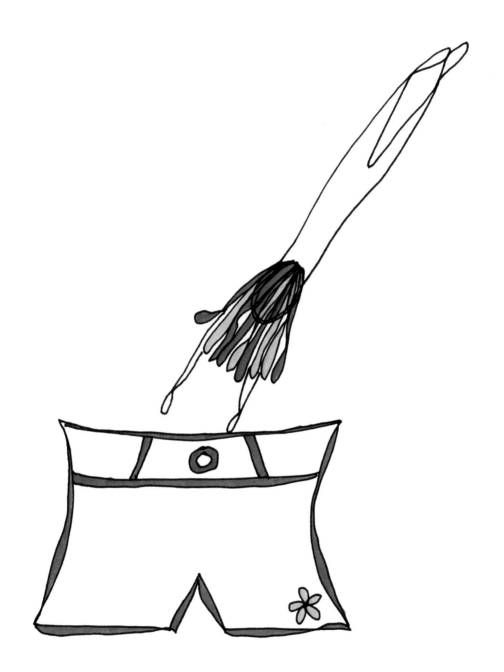

i forget the pool opens later
on tuesdays. i now sit
outside the locked door
in my oopsa daisy. this is
clearly part of today's swim...

allowing even this moment

to find + form me ✿

chlorine is drying out my
hair. there are costs
for being all in. there
are trade-offs for
everything. there
is wear + tear as i
wrestle myself into
full swim ✳

this morning's lifeguard played
music on her boom box.
the sound filled the pool
room. like a flying fish,
i kept surfacing. only for
me, it was for notes. we
all leap for what we need,
yes? + bring it back into
the water ✿

it is
comforting
to see
my hands
move
underwater
because it
reminds me
that even
though i
am someplace
else, i am
right here ✿

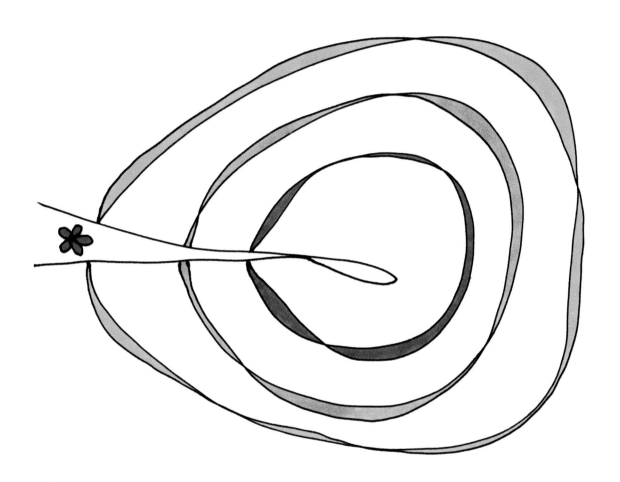

this whole swim is a
succession of high fives.
with each stroke, my hand
+water meet. i don't
have to be perfect. as
long as my arm comes
around + i keep kicking,
the deeps are there to
encourage me to make it
to the other side ✸

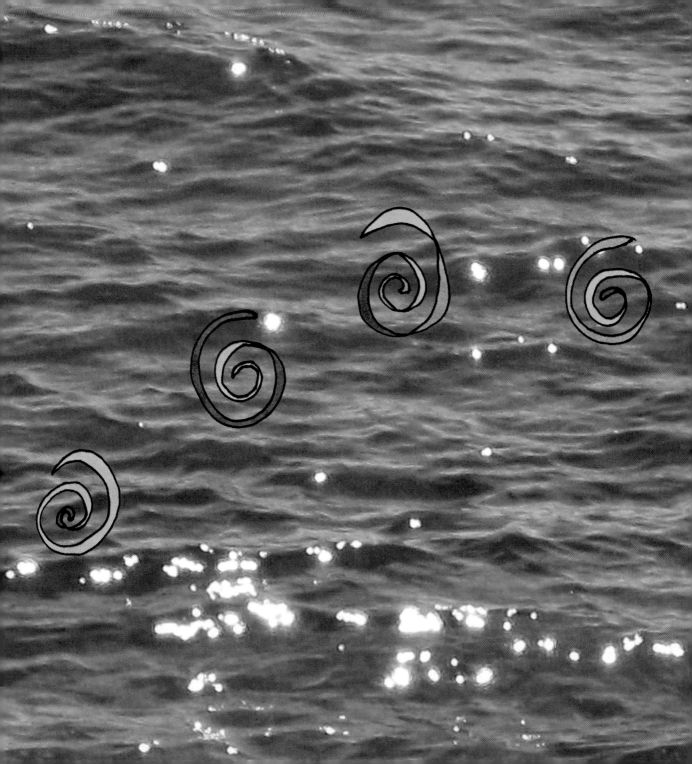

people say they want to
move toward the light
when they die. today
i am captured by the
light all over the pool
floor + swim in it.
i want to be here
as i live, too *

something fell away from
me in the water. what binds.
holds down. doesn't fit.
all i've outgrown. it
fell away just like that
+ it wasn't my plan.
this is what happens
when i swim the swim
that is mine to swim.
i let the all that is beautiful
do its job on me ✲

i usually try to swim fast in the last lap to build endurance or strength or something i was encouraged to do a long time ago + today i realized i could do anything in my last lap + in the middle of it, i did a front flip. it made me a little dizzy but i also felt more free ✿

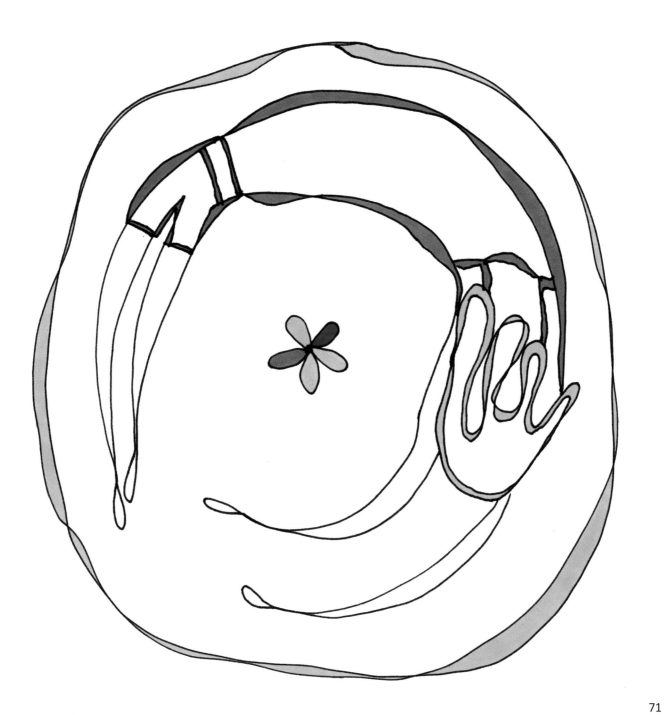

after the last lap,
i gently bent to
my knees at the
wall. tired, breathing
hard. i realized this
was prayer. holy.
holy. holy *

i hop up on the ledge at the end of today's swim. feet dangling in water. soaking it all in. i am here. i am here. i am here ❀

water gets in my ears +
i feel the full impact when
my swim is done. i tilt
my head to the side +
jump up + down. letting
go of all that doesn't
        belong *

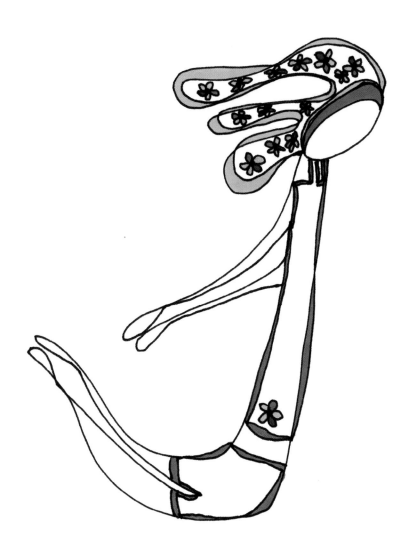

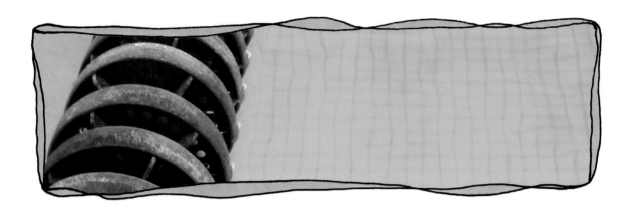

i told the person who got in
the swim lane i was just
in that it was a good lane
because i left her good joo
joo there + then i realized
that i am a jew + that is
maybe what we all hope to
do ~ leave behind the best
of ourselves for each other ❀

xox

i sang in the shower
after today's swim.
i wondered if
anyone could hear
me. the birds
don't seem to worry
about such things.
maybe i don't need
to either

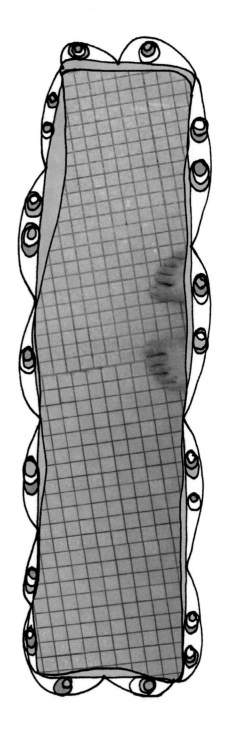

it is hard to put
my pants back on
after swimming.
i put my legs in +
my ankles stick,
still a little wet, before my
feet go all the way through
+ i stumble. "sit down +
do this," a quiet voice says
from within. "this doesn't
have to be so difficult. you
can give yourself what you need"

"my grandpa
gave me fins",

she said in the
locker room +
then i saw how

i've been given things

like breath + kick +
that everything allowing
us to move forward is
gift *

84

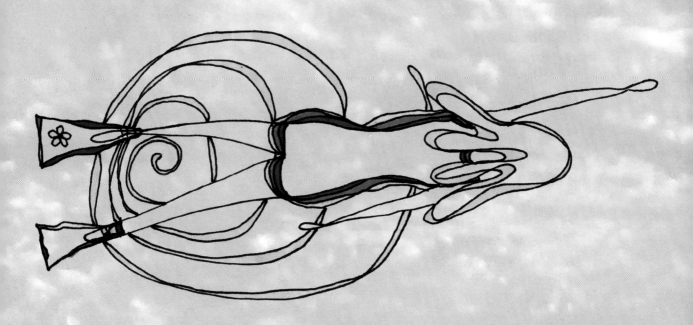

now that i am here, i
can brush my hand across
the water + send out
ripples to all of you.
"love", i say, quietly.
"love to all of you"...
brush, brush, brush

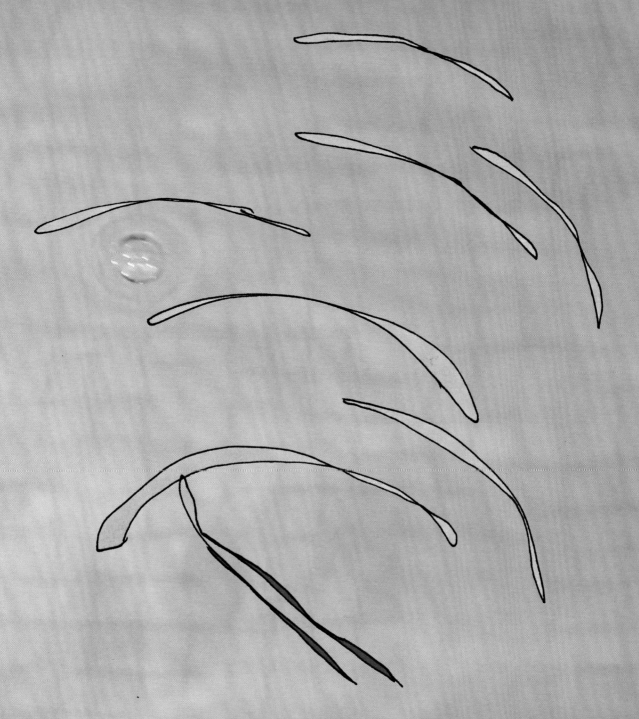

thank you

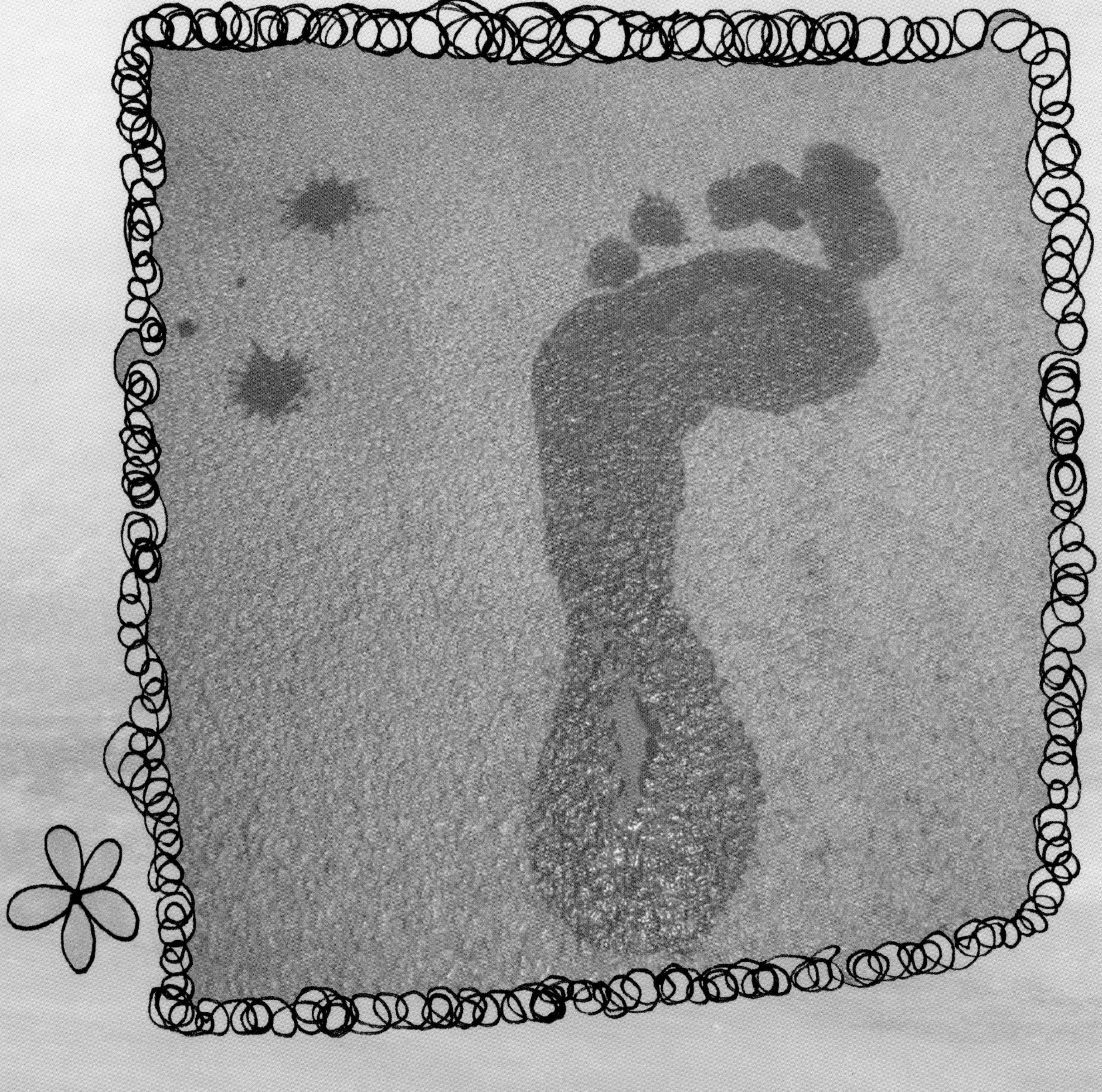

*dolphin

whale

everything
allowing us
to move
forward

water

singing birds

light

love

sank

raphael cushhir

brian andreas

loveliness

dreams

holiness

breath butterfly

tech wizard of ben awes

my oopsa daisies

the almost unseen

the deeps

rachel awes is available for signings + book readings

+ can be reached at rachelawes@gmail.com.